An Introduction to

Self-help for
Distressing Voices

An Introduction to
Self-help for
Distressing Voices

Cassie Hazell, Mark Hayward,
Clara Strauss and David Kingdon

ROBINSON

First published in Great Britain in 2018 by Robinson

1 3 5 7 9 10 8 6 4 2

A CIP catalogue record for this book
is available from the British Library.

Important note
This book is not intended as a substitute for medical advice
or treatment. Any person with a condition requiring medical
attention should consult a qualified medical practitioner
or suitable therapist.

ISBN: 978-1-47214-034-0

Typeset in Bembo by Initial Typesetting Services, Edinburgh
Printed and bound in Great Britain by CPI Group (UK) Ltd,
Croydon CR0 4YY.

Papers used by Robinson are from well-managed forests
and other responsible sources.

Contents

About this book

This book is for people who hear distressing voices. You may know these as auditory hallucinations. We have had invaluable help from the experts in this field to put this book together – people who themselves hear distressing voices. The book is broken down into specific topics, each related to an aspect of hearing voices that research shows can increase distress. The story of Martin will be used throughout the book to illustrate what can be learnt from each section that can help you with your voices. Whilst Martin is a fictional character, his experiences are similar to many people who are distressed by hearing voices. If you would like to find out more about the ideas in this book, you might find it helpful to read the accompanying self-help book called *Overcoming Distressing Voices* (Mark Hayward, Clara Strauss and David Kingdon, Robinson 2012).

At the end of each topic there is a 'Key Points' page that will cover all the things discussed. There is also a space for you to reflect on how you found the topic, what you found helpful and how you can put this into practice.

At the back of the book there are several diary pages (see page 136–7) that you can use to keep a track of what you have learnt and what you have done about it. You might like to photocopy this and use it to keep track of your progress as you work through this book.

Look out for headings that highlight certain helpful parts of the material:

Top tip

Tips from people who have previously used the book.

Q & A

Parts of the book featuring questions for you to think about and answer.

Using this book

The aim of this book is to reduce the negative impact that voices can have on your life. Sometimes voices go, but that's not the aim – voices are a bit like memories, they may fade, become less distressing but usually don't disappear altogether.

You can use this book in any way that is helpful to you – but here are a few tips from people who have used this book in the past:

Top tip

- Write things down – it can help to write down any ideas or thoughts you have while completing this book because you might forget things, think of something particularly clever or really useful, or might want to come back to something at a later date.

- Give it a go – some of the activities in this book

might feel difficult, but it can be worth it in the long term.

- Remember that it is *self*-help – completing the activities in this book will involve you dedicating some time and mental effort to it. As they say, the more you put into it, the more you get out.

- Try to complete the book in the order it is written – generally people have found it helpful to develop more effective coping strategies and increase their self-esteem, before trying to change beliefs about voices and standing up to them.

- Set yourself regular times to use the book or at least plan when you are next going to use it – it's very easy to let it drift, forget and then never get back to it.

- Do the activities more than once – it can be helpful to complete them several times on different occasions to help you learn and remember the lessons from each activity

- Involve others – you might find it helpful to discuss the activities in this book with other people, like family, or friends, and get them to remind you to use it.

- If you have a health worker, you might want to show them the book and see if they can help you with it.

- Keep yourself safe — if you find yourself getting overwhelmed or voices are getting too distressing while completing this book, please take a break and come back to it later on, and if necessary use your usual sources of support.

- Take the time to acknowledge your progress — you can use the diary pages in this book to make a note of any goals you have met or look back to see if anything has changed for you.

What is 'voice hearing'?

'Voice hearing' means hearing someone or something talking when nobody or nothing seems to be speaking.

Voice hearing is common to many different mental health problems. But lots of people who do not experience mental health problems hear voices too. Voices sound like somebody talking out loud and range from being quiet to very loud. They can make sense or seem like jumbled nonsense. They can also be confusing because other people say they don't hear what you are hearing. It can sometimes be hard to believe that other people cannot hear what you can, but usually there is someone you trust enough that can tell you whether they can hear the voices or not. If it is just you hearing the voices, then this experience can be called a 'hallucination'.

Voices can be difficult to explain: how can I hear someone talking when it's not coming from any person? Sometimes the voice may seem to be coming through walls or from a distance – it may sound like your neighbours or machinery or something else. You might want to check out whether the sound is coming from the place you think it is. If it seems that the voices aren't being spoken by somebody, it can still be helpful to try to work out what is causing them. It may take some time to come up with an explanation that makes sense and fits in with the other things happening to you. You may want to explore that explanation with others to see how reasonable it is.

Voices can arise for a lot of reasons. For example:

• Severe lack of sleep

• Bereavements

• Stress or traumatic experiences.

Hearing voices can often be a response to the things going on for you at the time – rather like dreams or nightmares – except these dreams don't switch off when you are awake.

When voices occur, the part of the brain that is responsible for processing 'speech' become active. It doesn't mean that there is anything wrong with the brain – just that the brain is reflecting what is going on.

Many famous people report hearing voices, including actor Anthony Hopkins and footballer Vinnie Jones. It is quite common for people to experience 'hallucinations' when they are very stressed, bereaved or sleeping poorly.

Everybody's experiences with voices are *different*:

- It can sometimes be reassuring as the voice can sound like a familiar person.

- It can sometimes be a pleasant experience that can relieve loneliness.

- It can be neutral – neither good nor bad, but still a little confusing.

- It can also be very distressing and disturbing.

This book is intended for this last group of people – those who are hearing voices and find the experience distressing.

Voices tend to be personal to the hearer in terms of their . . .

Content	• Some voices may say nasty things or talk about us in a negative way. • Some may say things that are personally meaningful. • Some may say things that are pleasant or comforting.
Location	• Some voices may be heard from a specific place (like the corner of the room) or heard 'on the air'. • Sometimes they may come from within our body.
Frequency	• Some voices may be fleeting and disappear with time. • Some voices may last longer. • Some voices may speak constantly whilst others speak only occasionally.
Identity	• Some people can hear a single voice and others can hear many voices. • We may recognise a voice as someone that we know – maybe from our past – and some voices may not be familiar at all.

Whilst it may not be possible to make voices go away for everybody who hears them, there are lots of ways to make these experiences more manageable. The activities in this book are designed to help you reduce the distress associated with hearing voices.

Martin's story

Martin is forty-four and lives on his own in a flat in London. He grew up with his parents and older sister and remembers seeing his parents constantly arguing. On one occasion, he saw his father hit his mother in front of him. When he was five, his father left the family home and he didn't see him again. Martin's mother remarried a couple of years later but, unfortunately, this was also an abusive relationship, with his mother frequently being beaten. As Martin became older he would try to protect his mother but this would only result in him being beaten as well. His mother ended the relationship when Martin was eleven. He continued to live with her until he was sixteen, when he left home to join the army. Unfortunately, Martin was bullied while in the army and, when he was eighteen, he started to hear voices for the first time and was medically discharged.

He heard the voice of his stepfather telling him he was weak, unable to defend himself and that he deserved all he got from the bullies. The voice told him he was no good and worthless and that no one would ever love him. The voice was around every day, although not all the time. When the voice first started Martin felt terrified and stayed indoors as much as possible. He avoided seeing friends and his mother and sister. He believed the voice was his stepfather communicating with him – and he believed that what the voice said about him was true.

Martin has not worked consistently since being discharged from the army. Despite having a series of jobs, his difficulties with the voices have led him to taking time off sick and either leaving jobs of his own accord or being sacked. He lost contact with his childhood friends but sees his mother and sister regularly. He continues to hear the voice of his stepfather, which as well as making derogatory comments also makes threats to harm Martin. Martin still believes everything the voice says and believes that the voice has the power to harm him. Understandably, he feels frightened, has difficulty sleeping and tries to cope by having the TV switched on twenty-four hours a day. He uses this as a way of drowning out the voice. In the past he used alcohol to try to cope, but he has not had a drink for seven years.

Here's how Martin describes hearing his voices:

'The voices are really distressing and they're difficult to cope with some days and I find it difficult to go out when they're really bad. Sometimes I feel really anxious and panicky and even have panic attacks.

'When you hear voices it's very lonely as it's not really something you can talk about to your friends and family. It's something you sort of have to endure on your own really and it's quite often isolating.'

Martin's description is a powerful reminder of the way some people can react to hearing voices. If you have noticed any of these reactions in yourself, it is important to remember that they are very common and that things can get better. Indeed, Martin has gone on to recover and we will follow him on his journey of recovery throughout the rest of this book.

Part 1: Coping

1

Coping with voices

Within this first topic, we will look at different ways of coping with distressing voices. While change is about taking steps to make things better – reducing the distress caused by voices – coping is more about taking steps to stop things from getting worse. This difference between coping and change may seem unimportant, but can in fact create stepping-stones towards being in a better place with our voices.

We can think about coping with voices in two ways:

What happens *before* voices start?	What happens *after* voices start?
Are there certain situations where you are more likely to hear distressing voices?	How do you respond to voices when they're around?
Are there certain situations where you feel more distressed by your voices?	What coping strategies do you use when voices start talking?
Are there certain feelings that regularly trigger distressing voices?	How helpful are these coping strategies?

Before the voices:
what are the triggers?

Voices can sometimes be predictable and occur at certain **times**, in certain **places** or when you are **feeling** a particular way. For example:

Time: night-time is often reported as a time when voices can be more active and distressing. Also, voices may become more difficult to manage when you are less active and there are fewer things to distract you.

Places: voices may also occur and become more distressing in certain rooms at home or when you go out and enter crowded places.

Feelings: voices can also occur when negative feelings are around, like when you are feeling stressed, down or really tired.

It can be helpful to become more aware of the patterns of voice activity. If you know when and where your voices are more likely to occur and to be distressing, you can be prepared to use your coping strategies.

Try answering the questions below – noting the times and places where voices occur, and your feelings at these times.

Q & A

What are the **times of day** when voices are active, or feel more distressing?

_____

_____

_____

_____

What are the **places** where voices are active, or feel more distressing?

_____

_____

_____

_____

What **feelings** are around before voices start talking?

_____

_____

_____

_____

Is there anything else you can think of that can trigger the voice(s)?

_____

_____

_____

_____

As we have seen, in addition to certain times of day or places triggering voices, voices can be triggered by negative feelings. If you can find helpful ways to manage negative feelings and prevent them from becoming extreme, this may help you to cope better with your voices.

There is no one right way to manage negative feelings – different things work for different people. Some ideas to manage negative feelings and stress include:

- Taking a warm bath

- Progressive muscle relaxation (tensing and then relaxing your muscles, starting at your feet and working up the body)

- Listening to music

- Exercise

- Finding a quiet place

- Regular sleeping habits (going to bed and getting up at the same times each day).

Any other ideas that work for you?

_____

_____

_____

_____

_____

_____

_____

> **Top tip**

If you are finding it difficult to think of ideas for ways to manage stress you might find it helpful to research what other people who hear voices have found helpful. For example, mental health internet forums (e.g. www.hearing-voices.org), mental health Facebook groups (e.g. Drop the Disorder), or YouTube videos (e.g. search on 'hearing voices network').

3

After voices: coping strategies

After your voices have started talking or when they become distressing, how do you respond? Do you try to ignore voices or distract yourself by listening to music, watching TV or keeping yourself busy? Do you sometimes talk back to the voices and try to argue with them? Maybe you have tried a lot of different strategies over time – some that worked well and others that didn't? There are no 'magic' strategies!

The goal of this topic is to explore ways to make your coping strategies more helpful, and identify if any could be making voices worse.

How can you make your coping strategies more helpful?

| Can they be tweaked to increase their helpfulness? | Can you start to use your coping strategies before the voices become too distressing? | Can you use any of your coping strategies more often? |

(*Top tip*)

Here are some examples of how people have made their coping strategies more effective:

1. Listening to music through headphones as soon as voices start.

2. More regularly engaging in enjoyable and/or fulfilling activities that can help to focus attention; e.g. playing computer games, doing a hobby or socialising with other people.

3. Being equipped to use strategies at triggering times, e.g. having headphones available when going out into crowds.

Martin's story

> Martin listens to rock music on his iPod when his voices are troubling him. This helps him to cope as the music drowns out the voice. Martin can also get lost in the music and tune out of what the voice is saying.

It's important to consider if any of your coping strategies are accidentally making things worse in any way. We often respond very instinctively to voices – like a reflex. For example, we might instinctively start talking back to voices and before we realise it's happening we are arguing and feeling more upset. Also, sometimes coping strategies that seem helpful in the short term can make things worse in the long term – e.g. staying at home and avoiding people might help in the short term but might limit your quality of life in the long term.

Do any of your strategies make things worse? Could any of your strategies make things worse in the long term? If yes, can you stop using this strategy or use this strategy less often, e.g. try not to talk back to voices – and see what happens?

How can coping strategies make things worse?

Do any of your coping strategies make voices more distressing?

Do any of your coping strategies help in the short term, but make things worse in the long term?

Do any of your coping strategies make voices last longer?

> ### Top tip

Here are some examples of coping strategies that people were using, but were making voices worse in the long term:

1. Becoming angry and arguing with voices.

2. Trying to ignore them rather than accepting and coping with them.

3. Drinking excessive amounts of alcohol.

4. Taking illegal drugs.

> ### Q & A

You may find it useful to use the questions below to help you think about your current coping strategies. You can tell a coping strategy is working if it makes you feel more able to cope with voices and give you a greater sense of control.

How do you respond to voices when they start talking (e.g. distracting, ignoring, talking back, relaxing)?

_____

_____

_____

_____

When do you use the coping strategies (e.g. times, places, situations)?

_____

_____

_____

_____

How **helpful** are these coping strategies?

0	1	2	3	4	5	6	7	8	9	10

Not at all   Extremely

Do any of these coping strategies make voices worse (e.g. shouting back can sometimes lead to voices getting louder) or make you feel worse?

_____

_____

_____

_____

Do any of these coping strategies help in the short term, but make things worse in the longer term?

_____

_____

_____

_____

Is there a coping strategy that you could use more often/differently? What will you do and when?

_____

_____

_____

_____

When you've tried your coping strategy, check how effective it was:

• It may not have solved the problem but did it help just a little?

- Could you have done it differently?

- Is it worth using it again?

- Or trying something different?

_____

_____

_____

_____

Spending time with other people can be a useful strategy for coping with voices. Being with other people can keep our minds occupied and take our attention away from voices.

Some ideas on how to socialise more are:

- Do something positive with others, e.g. go for a walk, go for a coffee, play a game, watch a sports match, watch a TV programme, or go see a film.

- Talk to others who seem understanding about your voices.

- Take up an old hobby.

- Call an old friend.

• Look for a new interest.

• Try online social networking sites that are run by mental health organisations.

• Work activities both in and outside the home.

• Any other ideas?

_____

_____

_____

_____

Martin's story

Martin uses Facebook to stay in touch with friends that he used to spend time with. He is thinking about asking to meet with some of these old friends, but he feels quite nervous about doing this. He is concerned about how the voices will react.

Top tip

Mental health care

Talking to a mental health worker who understands voice hearing experiences can be hugely beneficial.

There is also medication. It can help people who hear distressing voices. Sometimes varying the dose can be helpful (please discuss any changes in medication with your therapist or doctor in the first instance).

Medication is not always helpful for everyone and side effects can be a problem – and nobody wants to take medication if they don't need it. So if you are not sure that it is helping, do speak with the person prescribing it and explain your situation so that you can weigh up the advantages and disadvantages of continuing. Even if you disagree about the value of medication, it is important to keep contact with your health worker – work out the early signs that your mental health might be getting worse so that you can do something quickly. That doesn't mean automatically increasing or going back on medication. Have a discussion with your health worker can help you to work out how best to manage things.

Finding a coping strategy that works for you can involve some **persistence**, and **trial and error**. Everyone is different, and is therefore likely to find different coping strategies more or less helpful.

4

Key points

- It can help to become more aware of the times, places and feelings that can trigger distressing voices.

- It can also be useful to look in detail at your current ways of coping with distressing voices. Which of your coping strategies are most helpful? Are there any that are unhelpful? Are there any that are helpful in the short term, but unhelpful in the longer term?

- Can you tweak your current coping strategies to increase the benefit you get from them?

- Can you try some different coping strategies in order to find additional strategies that work for you?

- Do think about and discuss your use of medication – whether you are taking medication or, if not, could it help? Consider the pros and cons of taking medication so that you can use it most effectively.

• Keep a record of your different ways of trying to cope and keep monitoring their effectiveness.

Notes

_____

_____

_____

_____

_____

_____

_____

_____

Reflecting on the Coping topic

After working through this topic you might find it helpful to take some time to reflect on what you might have learnt. There is space for you to write an answer in relation to each of these questions, as well as space for you to add your own reflections.

How have you found this topic?	What have you learnt from this topic?
_____	_____
_____	_____
_____	_____
_____	_____
_____	_____
_____	_____
What is one good thing you can take away from this topic?	**What positive action could you take over the next week?**
_____	_____
_____	_____
_____	_____
_____	_____
_____	_____
_____	_____
_____	_____

Personal reflections

_____

_____

_____

_____

_____

Part 2: Me

5

Playing the curious detective

Over the next two topics you will be asked to identify the beliefs that you have about yourself and your voices. You will be invited to consider whether these beliefs are helpful or not. If you decide that they are not helpful then you might want to check the accuracy of these beliefs.

This is where you will need to play the curious detective who finds and interrogates the evidence that proves or disproves your beliefs but . . .

BEWARE OF THE CONFIRMATION BIAS!

What is the confirmation bias?

People are more likely to look for and remember information that supports their beliefs and less likely to consider information that does not support the belief. This is the confirmation bias.

Let's look again at Martin . . .

Martin's story

One of Martin's negative beliefs about himself is, 'I am stupid.'

He developed this view of himself as a young child, seemingly based on good reasons: he struggled to read and write at primary school and noticed other children doing things he couldn't do. Martin also had a teacher who kept telling him to try harder. When he was eight years old, he was diagnosed as being very short-sighted and started to wear glasses. Once this happened, his reading and writing caught up with the level achieved by his friends. However, by this point, his belief – 'I am stupid' – was firmly rooted in his mind.

As an adult, Martin became very good at noticing reasons why this belief was true, for instance when he failed his first driving test. He also would sit and think about reasons why this belief must be true – and he would remember the critical comments from his former teacher. The more reasons Martin noticed to support his belief, the more he believed it must be true.

The other thing we all tend to do is **ignore evidence** that does not support our beliefs. For instance,

Martin didn't change his belief 'I am stupid' when he passed his driving test the second time around. Another thing that some of us do is **twist evidence** to fit with our beliefs. So, rather than Martin taking pleasure from his friend telling him how much he valued their friendship, Martin would think, my friends feel sorry for me because I am stupid.

For all these reasons, once we develop a belief it tends to become stronger over time as we search for evidence that supports it, ignore evidence that does not support it and even twist evidence to make it fit.

This confirmation bias can become a problem when we are maintaining unhelpful beliefs that might not be true. Try to keep this in mind and play the '**curious detective**' – look at the evidence and question your beliefs.

6

Self-esteem

We all have ideas and opinions about the kind of person we are. Low self-esteem is when our overall view of ourselves is negative – when we have negative beliefs about who we are as a person. Low self-esteem and hearing distressing voices tend to go hand-in-hand. To find out if low self-esteem is a problem for you, you might find it helpful to complete the Rosenberg Self-Esteem Scale[1] below. Just choose the option that best applies to you, then add up your score.

		Strongly agree	Agree	Disagree	Strongly disagree
1	On the whole I am satisfied with myself	3	2	1	0
2	At times, I think I am no good at all	0	1	2	3

1 *Society and the Adolescent Self-Image*, Rosenberg M., Princeton University Press; 1965

3	I feel that I have a number of good qualities	3	2	1	0
4	I am able to do things as well as most other people	3	2	1	0
5	I feel I do not have much to be proud of	0	1	2	3
6	I certainly feel useless at times	0	1	2	3
7	I feel that I'm a person of worth, at least on an equal plane with others	3	2	1	0
8	I wish I could have more respect for myself	0	1	2	3
9	All in all, I am inclined to feel that I am a failure	0	1	2	3
10	I take a positive attitude towards myself	3	2	1	0
	Sub-total:				
	My total score is:				

Most people score around 22 or 23. If you score lower than this then you might have lower self-esteem than most.

7

Core beliefs

There are lots of reasons why someone might have low self-esteem and most people begin to develop it during childhood. People who hear voices are particularly likely to have had difficult early life experiences.

To understand why you have a low self-esteem it can be helpful to identify your core beliefs. Core beliefs are phrased as 'I am . . .' statements, and are beliefs that are thought to be true all the time (i.e. don't change depending on the situation). They can be both positive and negative. If you have low self-esteem you will most likely have more negative core beliefs than positive ones.

Examples of positive core beliefs	Examples of negative core beliefs
'I am worthwhile'	'I am stupid'
'I am friendly'	'I am weak'
'I am kind'	'I am unlikeable'

Core beliefs can become stronger over time because of the confirmation bias that we looked at earlier – we all have a tendency to remember and notice evidence that fits with and supports our beliefs. We also tend to ignore the evidence that goes against our beliefs. This means that we can end up remembering lots of evidence that supports our core beliefs and forgetting evidence that doesn't support our core beliefs. This can make it easier for us to carry on believing them.

If we believe negative things about ourselves then it is also easier to believe that our voices have power and control over us and that any unpleasant comments they make are true. If you have found that you might have a problem with low self-esteem you might find it helpful to try and identify a negative core belief and consider how this core belief affects you.

You may find that your negative core belief is very like, even identical, to a distressing thing that the voices say, e.g. 'you're useless' which then makes you feel 'I'm useless'.

In response to some very difficult early life experiences, Martin came to the conclusion that he was weak and vulnerable, no good and not worth anything. For this exercise Martin has chosen to work on his belief that he is weak and vulnerable.

Negative core belief to work on: 'I am weak and vulnerable.'

Top tip

Remember to play the curious detective, and be-ware of the confirmation bias (see pages 27–9 to learn more about this). If you are having trouble with this topic it can help to get some support from someone with a more objective view, e.g. friends, family or health professionals.

The negative core belief that I hold about myself is that . . .

'I am _____'

How certain are you that this negative core belief is true?

'Right *now* I believe this core belief is true with about ___ % certainty.'

What impact does this negative core belief have on you?

I feel . . . Name the feeling in one word	Strength of feeling (per cent), where 100 per cent means the feeling is as strong as possible	Bodily sensations Do you notice anything in your body when you feel this way?

8

Searching for evidence

Beliefs are *not* the same as facts; they are best guesses. The confirmation bias might lead us to miss some important evidence when we are arriving at this guess. It can be helpful to take the time to look at all of the available evidence, as this will enable you to feel more confident about the accuracy of your guesses.

Taking the negative core belief you identified previously, start to think of evidence and experiences that would mean this belief is not completely true all of the time.

Top tip

You might find this difficult so try to think about different times in your life or ask family and friends if they can think of any examples. We're interested in small things as well as big things.

Evidence and experiences that meant this negative core belief is not completely true all the time . . .
1
2
3
4
5
6
7
8
9
10

After reviewing the evidence, how certain are you that this negative core belief is true?

'Right *now* I believe this core belief is true with about_____ % certainty.'

Martin's story

Martin's negative core belief: 'I am weak and vulnerable.'

Evidence and experiences that mean this negative core belief is not completely true all of the time.

1. I live on my own and manage without help from anyone.

2. I joined the army and completed the training: some other people had to drop out.

3. I am physically quite strong.

Q & A

Has your certainty of your belief changed at all?

Yes / no

If it has changed, did your certainty increase or decrease?

Increase / decrease

If your certainty in the belief has **decreased**, then this is great − so keep collecting evidence!

If your certainty in the belief has **increased**, then this might mean the confirmation bias has crept in − you might find it helpful to review the evidence and check whether the evidence shows that this belief is not completely true all of the time.

If your certainty is the **same**, then this is totally understandable − core beliefs have generally been around for a long time so it can take some time to change them.

Top tip

It can take time to gather all the evidence that will enable you to confidently assess the accuracy of your core beliefs. You can continue to add to this list over time as you come across more examples of your negative core belief not being completely true all the time.

If you have found this helpful, then you might want to repeat this process with another negative core belief. This will involve:

1. Identifying a negative core belief.

2. Rating your certainty that this belief is true.

3. Searching for evidence that shows the negative core belief is not completely true all of the time.

4. Rating how certain you are that this belief is true after reviewing the evidence.

5. If your certainty in the belief has not reduced, then it might be helpful to review the evidence, collect more or ask others for help collecting evidence.

9

Alternative beliefs that are more helpful

Core beliefs have developed over a long period of time so, like any strong beliefs, they may take some time before there is any sign of them changing. You might find it helpful to continue looking for evidence for and against your negative core beliefs or you might want to try this exercise with another negative core belief.

As well as re-examining our negative core beliefs, we can try to strengthen alternative, more helpful beliefs in order to try and boost our self-esteem. Try to think of an alternative, more helpful core belief that you might feel is a little bit true or would like to feel about yourself. Then try to think of evidence for and against this belief. It is usually easier to think of reasons why it is not true – so you might have to work a little harder to think of reasons why it is true.

Top tip

Don't dismiss something because it seems too insignificant, e.g. 'helped my parents/partner with cleaning the room/doing the shopping'. These all build up to a picture of you trying to do be positive and do your best.

Here are some examples of alternative beliefs you might want to use . . .

'I am worthy of respect', 'I am valuable', 'I am talented', 'I am successful', 'I am good', 'I am interesting'.

Top tip

If you have low self-esteem it can be difficult to think of alternative beliefs. Instead, it can be easier to think about what positive things other people might say about you – e.g. what would your family/friends/neighbour/health professional say if you asked them to identify an alternative belief about you?

Martin's alternative, more helpful belief: 'I am likeable'.

Evidence and experiences that support this belief:

1. Pete keeps coming around; I guess he wouldn't if he didn't like me.

2. I treat people pretty well and try not to offend anyone.

3. The woman in the shop is always really friendly to me and asks how I am.

Top tip

It also might be helpful to think back to a time when your self-esteem was a little higher – what were some of the alternative beliefs you held about yourself then?

The alternative belief that I want to strengthen is that...

'I am _____.'

How certain are you that this alternative belief is true?

'Right *now* I believe this alternative belief is true with about_____ % certainty.'

Now start to think of evidence and experiences that **support** this alternative belief i.e. show that this belief might be true, or is true some/all of the time. Remember, we are interested in the small things as well as big things.

Evidence and experiences that support the alternative belief . . .
1
2
3
4
5
6

7	
8	
9	
10	

Beliefs not only affect the way we *feel* about ourselves, they can also influence the way we *behave*.

Looking at your alternative belief, can you think of the ways you would behave differently if it were true? Try to think of some ideas and make a note of them here.

Top tip

You might find it easier to consider this question from another angle: what is your low self-esteem stopping you from doing? If you didn't have low self-esteem what would you be doing that is different from how things are now?

If I believed my alternative beliefs with 100% certainty I would be . . .

1	
2	
3	
4	
5	

Once you have identified some actions, why not try them out? If we act like our alternative belief is true then this can help us to believe it more of the time. This might seem scary at first, so maybe just try to make a small change at first. You can think of this as 'testing out' your new alternative belief.

You might find it helpful to make a note of specific things that you could do and when you could do them. It might be helpful to start with a small change and then build on this when you feel ready.

Q & A

What can I do to test out my alternative belief?

_____

_____

_____

_____

_____

_____

_____

Martin's story

> Martin's alternative, more helpful belief: 'I am likeable.'
>
> If I believed this was true with 100% certainty I would be . . .
>
> 1. Calling Pete and asking about meeting up, not just waiting for him to come around all the time.
>
> 2. Trying to find more of my old friends on Facebook and getting back in touch.
>
> 3. Smiling at people more (in shops and other places).

Once you have had a go at gathering evidence to support your alternative belief and tried testing it out you might want to ask yourself again how much you believe your alternative belief and see if there has been any change.

After reviewing the evidence, how certain are you that this alternative belief is true?

'Right *now* I believe this core belief is true with about ___ % certainty.'

Q & A

Has your certainty of your belief changed at all?

Yes / no

If it has changed, did your certainty increase or decrease?

Increase / decrease

If your certainty in the belief has **increased**, then this is great – so keep collecting evidence!

If your certainty in the belief has **decreased**, then this might mean the confirmation bias has crept in – you might find it helpful to review the evidence and check whether the evidence supports your alternative belief.

If your certainty is the **same**, then this is totally understandable – low self-esteem can make it difficult for us to believe positive things about ourselves, so it can take time to break this habit.

If you have found this helpful, then you might want to repeat this process with another alternative, more helpful belief. This will involve:

1. Identifying an alternative belief.

2. Rating how certain you are that this belief is true.

3. Searching for evidence that supports this alternative belief.

4. Testing it out by acting like this belief is true.

5. Rating how certain you are that this belief is true after reviewing the evidence and testing it out.

6. If your certainty in the belief has not reduced, then it might be helpful to review the evidence, collect more or ask others for help collecting evidence.

10

Key Points

- If we believe negative things about ourselves then it is easier to believe that the voices we hear have power and control over us and that any unpleasant comments they make about us are true.

- We can begin to overcome low self-esteem by evaluating the accuracy of our negative core beliefs – our negative ideas about ourselves can seem true but they may not really be true.

- Another way of overcoming low self-esteem is to notice and build-up alternative, more helpful beliefs about ourselves.

- We can remind ourselves that negative thoughts and comments by voices are not necessarily true.

- As we begin to overcome low self-esteem, we might notice that it is easier to question the negative things the voices say and to pay them less attention.

• Overcoming low self-esteem is an important step on the road to overcoming distressing voices.

Notes

_____

_____

_____

_____

_____

_____

_____

_____

_____

Reflecting on the Me topic

After working through this topic you might find it helpful to take some time to reflect on what you might have learnt. There is space for you to write an answer in relation to each of these questions, as well as space for you to add your own reflections.

How have you found this topic?	What have you learnt from this topic?
_____	_____
_____	_____
_____	_____
_____	_____
_____	_____
_____	_____
What is one good thing you can take away from this topic?	**What positive action could you take over the next week?**
_____	_____
_____	_____
_____	_____
_____	_____
_____	_____
_____	_____

Personal reflections

_____

_____

_____

_____

_____

Part 3: My voices

11

Beliefs about voices

We have previously played the curious detective by evaluating the accuracy of our negative beliefs about ourselves. We will now take the same approach to explore the accuracy of the beliefs we have about our voices.

Although everybody's experience of hearing voices is different, there tend to be common types of beliefs that many people hold about their voices. The three most common beliefs about voices are as follows:

1. Omnipotence	• This relates to our beliefs about the voice's **power**. • Often people believe that the voice is **all-powerful**.
2. Malevolence	• This relates to our beliefs about the voice's **intentions**. • It is common for people to believe the voice has **bad intentions**.

3. Omniscience	• This relates to our belief about how **truthful** we think the voice is. • The voice's comments can make it seem as if it is **all-knowing**.

If a person believes a voice is all-powerful, all-knowing and has bad intentions this will make the voice more distressing in comparison with a voice that is seen as powerless or having good intentions.

Cognitive behavioural therapy (CBT)

CBT for hearing voices is based around the idea that when someone hears a voice, the way they feel and behave will be affected by their beliefs about the voices. The diagram opposite can help to explain how CBT works using the ABC model.

Activating event
Hearing a voice or voices

Beliefs and thoughts about the activating event
Beliefs about voices, myself, other people and the world

Consequences of 'A' and 'B' above
Common responses to voices

These can be:

Behaviours

Feelings

Bodily
sensations

The ABC model shows that our beliefs about an event can lead to different consequences. This means that two people can experience the same activating event, but experience different consequences.

Here is an example to demonstrate how beliefs can influence consequences. Let's look at the beliefs that Martin has developed about his voices and their consequences, and compare this to Sarah.

In this diagram you can see that two people can have the same **A**ctivating event, but their **B**eliefs are different. The difference in the beliefs can lead to different **C**onsequences. In order to influence the consequences we need to think about and re-evaluate our beliefs. CBT techniques can help us to do this.

Identifying beliefs about voices

The first step is to identify what you think about your voices. Before you do this, choose one particular voice to focus on. If you hear two or more voices it might be best to choose the voice that you want to change the most. If you hear a crowd of voices then choose a belief you have about the crowd.

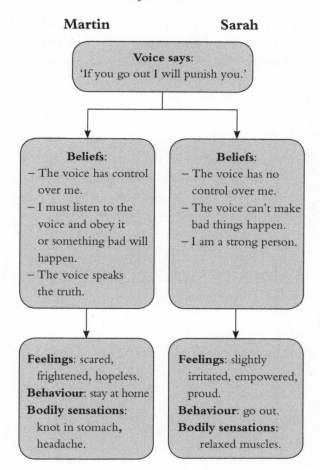

Martin   **Sarah**

Voice says:
'If you go out I will punish you.'

Beliefs:
- The voice has control over me.
- I must listen to the voice and obey it or something bad will happen.
- The voice speaks the truth.

Beliefs:
- The voice has no control over me.
- The voice can't make bad things happen.
- I am a strong person.

Feelings: scared, frightened, hopeless.
Behaviour: stay at home
Bodily sensations: knot in stomach, headache.

Feelings: slightly irritated, empowered, proud.
Behaviour: go out.
Bodily sensations: relaxed muscles.

It can be difficult to work out what we think about our voices. You might find completing this questionnaire developed by Chadwick, Lees and

Birchwood[2] a helpful way to identify your beliefs. A higher score means a stronger belief in the power and control of the voice or its harmful intentions.

> **Top tip**

Voices might try to influence your answers to the questionnaire below, so try your best to separate what they think from what you believe. It is important to identify what *you* believe about your voices, not what voices want you to think or believe.

		Dis-agree	Unsure	Slightly agree	Strongly agree
1	My voice is very powerful	0	1	2	3
2	My voice seems to know everything about me	0	1	2	3
3	My voice makes me do things I really don't want to do	0	1	2	3
4	I cannot control my voice	0	1	2	3

---

2 'The Revised Beliefs About Voices Questionnaire (BAVQ-R)', Chadwick P., Lees S. and Birchwood M., *Br J Psychiatry*, 2000;177(SEPT):229–232.

| 5 | My voice will harm or kill me if I disobey or resist it | 0 | 1 | 2 | 3 |
| 6 | My voice rules my life | 0 | 1 | 2 | 3 |

The rating of my belief about my voice's power and control is _____ /18

		Dis-agree	Unsure	Slightly agree	Strongly agree
1	My voice is punishing me for something I have done	0	1	2	3
2	My voice is persecuting me for no good reason	0	1	2	3
3	My voice is evil	0	1	2	3
4	My voice wants to do harm	0	1	2	3
5	My voice wants me to do bad things	0	1	2	3
6	My voice is trying to corrupt or destroy me	0	1	2	3

The rating of my belief about my voice's harmful intentions is _____ /18

Q & A

How did you get on?

What did you learn about your beliefs, and the power, control and intentions of your voices?

_____

_____

_____

_____

_____

_____

We can use the ABC model to look at what we think about our voices in more detail and understand the consequences of this. You can use the diagram below to do this.

Activating event

What does my voice say?

Beliefs and thoughts about the activating event

For each statement delete as appropriate:

I believe my voice is very powerful / quite powerful / a bit powerful / not at all powerful.

I believe my voice controls me completely / quite a lot / a bit / not at all.

Consequences of A & B

How does my voice make me feel and behave?

Feelings:

Behaviours:

After completing these exercises, you may have noticed that you have some negative beliefs related to voices. You might find it helpful to take the time to think about the beliefs you have and decide which one you would like to work on.

If you are finding it difficult to choose, it might help to remind yourself of the most common types of negative beliefs that people can have about their voices . . .

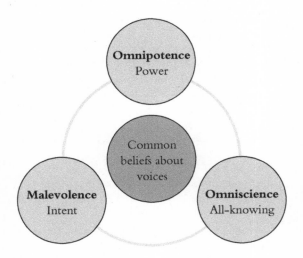

The belief about my voices that I want to work on is that . . .

'I believe my voice is _____'

I feel... Name the feeling in one word	Strength of feeling (%) Where a hundred per cent means the feeling is as strong as possible	Bodily sensations Do you notice anything in your body when you feel this way?		

How certain are you that this belief about your voice is true?

'Right *now* I believe this belief about my voices is true with about _____ % certainty.'

What impact does this belief about your voice have on you? You can use the information that you put into the ABC model to fill this in.

12

Searching for evidence

CBT is not about positive thinking, but rather about carefully and accurately analysing evidence. We need to ask ourselves, 'Is there any evidence that does not fit with our belief about the voice?'

Taking the belief about your voice you decided to work on, write down any evidence or experiences that mean the belief you have chosen is **not** completely true all the time. Remember, we are interested in the small things as well big things.

| Top tip |

To help you do this you might want to look back over the whole time during which you have been hearing voices and also consider whether you are giving yourself the chance to find evidence that will help you re-evaluate your belief.

Finding evidence can be a little tricky, especially if voices make it difficult for you to think clearly. To help you find evidence, here are some prompts:

- Have there been times when voices made predictions and they weren't one hundred per cent accurate?

- Have there been times when voices said things that weren't one hundred per cent accurate?

- Have there been times when voices haven't followed through with their threats?

- Have there been times when you haven't done what voices have told you to?

Martin's story

Martin's belief about his voice: 'I believe my voice is very powerful.'

Evidence and experiences that mean this belief is not completely true all of the time.

1. Occasionally I have not obeyed the voice and nothing terrible has happened.

2. My voice has never actually carried out any of its threats.

3. I went out yesterday and nothing bad happened to me.

Evidence and experiences that mean this belief about voices is not completely true all the time . . .
1
2
3
4
5
6
7
8
9
10

When you have collected your evidence you might want to ask yourself again how much you believe this belief.

Before you make your decision, take time to think about all the evidence that you have gathered.

After reviewing the evidence, how certain are you that this negative core belief is true?

'Right *now* I believe this core belief is true with about _____ % certainty.'

You might notice you believe this belief with less certainty now you have had the chance to gather evidence. On the other hand, you might notice you believe it just as strongly as you did at the start. If this happens you might want to spend more time finding new evidence or experiences, or try re-evaluating a different belief.

Q & A

Has your certainty of your belief changed at all?

Yes / no

If it has changed, did your certainty increase or decrease?

Increase / decrease

If your certainty in the belief has **decreased**, then this is great – so keep collecting evidence!

If your certainty in the belief has **increased**, then this might mean the confirmation bias has crept in – you might find it helpful to review the evidence and check whether the evidence shows that this belief is not completely true all of the time.

If your certainty is the **same**, then this is totally understandable – beliefs have generally been around for a long time so it can take some time to change them.

If you have found this helpful, then you might want to repeat this process with another belief that you have about your voice, or thinking about another voice that you hear. This will involve:

1. Identifying a belief you have about your voice.

2. Rating how certain you are that this belief is true.

3. Searching for evidence that shows the belief about your voices is not completely true all of the time.

4. Rating how certain you are that this belief is true after reviewing the evidence.

5. If your certainty in the belief has not reduced, then it might be helpful to review the evidence, collect more, or ask others for help collecting evidence.

Q & A

What other beliefs about my voices could I try to re-evaluate?

_____

_____

_____

_____

_____

_____

13

Key points

- If we believe our voices have power and control over us and want to harm us, this can be very distressing.

- However, beliefs are not facts; they are best guesses and can sometimes be wide of the mark.

- We can begin to overcome the distress caused by our voices by naming our beliefs about them and learning how these beliefs affect us.

- When we are familiar with these beliefs and their effects, we can re-evaluate the accuracy of our beliefs about our voices.

- We can re-evaluate the accuracy of our beliefs about our voices by gathering evidence that suggests that our beliefs are not true all of the time.

- After weighing up the evidence, we might conclude that our voices are less powerful than we previously thought and maybe we have more control than we thought.

• Re-evaluating our beliefs about our voices is one way to overcome our distressing voices. Another approach is to re-evaluate the beliefs we hold about ourselves.

Notes

_____

_____

_____

_____

_____

_____

_____

_____

Reflecting on the My Voices topic

After working through this topic you might find it helpful to take some time to reflect on what you might have learnt. There is space for you to write an answer in relation to each of these questions, as well as space for you to add your own reflections.

How have you found this topic?	What have you learnt from this topic?
_____	_____
_____	_____
_____	_____
_____	_____
_____	_____
_____	_____
What is one good thing you can take away from this topic?	**What positive action could you take over the next week?**
_____	_____
_____	_____
_____	_____
_____	_____
_____	_____
_____	_____

Personal reflections

_____

_____

_____

_____

_____

Part 4: My Relationships

14

Understanding relationships

Relationships are usually something that happens between two people. Relationships can be positive and supportive when they work well. But they can also be negative and a source of pain and distress.

We can think of relationships in two main ways:

Closeness   **and**   **Power**

Closeness	Power
Closeness refers to both the physical and emotional closeness within the relationship.	Power in a relationship means the amount of influence one person has over the other and how they use it.
Closeness can be negative. Someone may feel the other person is getting too close and interfering, is being too nosey or is too much in their space.	A negative use of power may result in one person trying to dominate the other, pushing them around or making them do something they don't want to – expecting them to give in.

15

Relationships with voices

Many people speak of having two-way conversations with their voice. There are similarities between the kinds of relationships that we can have with a person and with voices. Just like our social relationships, power and closeness are also important in understanding the relationship we have with voices.

It might seem a bit odd at first to think of yourself being in a relationship with your voices. It might help to think about the way you would describe your experience of hearing voices – could some of the language you use also be used to describe another person and your relationship with them?

To understand the **power** and **closeness** in your relationship with your voice you might find it helpful to fill in the questionnaire by Hayward and colleagues[3] below. The higher the score the more powerful and close you view your voice.

---

3 'The voice and You: Development and Psychometric Evaluation of a Measure of Relationships with Voices,' Hayward M., Denney J., Vaughan S. and Fowler D., *Clin Psychol Psychother.*, 2008;15(1):45-52.

		Nearly always true	Quite often true	Some-times true	Rarely true
1	My voice tries to get the better of me	3	2	1	0
2	My voice makes me feel useless	3	2	1	0
3	My voice tries to make me out to be stupid	3	2	1	0
4	My voice wants things done his/her way	3	2	1	0
5	My voice makes hurtful remarks to me	3	2	1	0
6	My voice constantly reminds me of my failings	3	2	1	0
7	My voice does not give me credit for the good things I do	3	2	1	0

The power rating for my voice is ____ /21

		Nearly always true	Quite often true	Some-times true	Rarely true
1	My voice finds it hard to allow me to have time away from him/her	3	2	1	0
2	My voice dislikes spending time on his/her own	3	2	1	0
3	My voice tries to accompany me when I go out	3	2	1	0
4	My voice dislikes it when I exclude him/her by showing an interest in other people	3	2	1	0
5	My voice does not let me have time to myself	3	2	1	0

The closeness rating for my voice is ___ /15

Q & A

Based on your answers to the question above:

How powerful does your voice seem to be?

_____

_____

How close does your voice seem to be?

_____

_____

Do you consider the power and/or the closeness in your relationship with your voice to be a problem?

_____

_____

_____

_____

_____

16

Responding to voices

You might now have an idea about how powerful and close you view your voice. It is common for voices to be rated as 'very powerful' and 'too close'.

Distressing voices tend to be seen as more powerful than the person who hears them. This power is often used in a negative way, for example by trying to dominate or intrude upon privacy.

There are lots of different ways that you can respond to voices. Some of the most common ways that people respond to their voices are listed below. Each of these responses is understandable and natural in the face of a threatening situation.

Try to escape

- If the distressing voice is too powerful or close we may deal with this by trying to create distance between us and the voice.

- Responding passively to voices is likely to strengthen any negative beliefs we have about the voice and ourselves.

Fight back

- A common reaction to powerful voices is to fight back.

- This can have negative consequences as the voice can become more aggressive in response to aggression.

Give in

- Giving in can be a sign of hopelessness.

- This can have a negative effect on self-esteem in the long term, and can strengthen negative beliefs about ourselves.

Q & A

Have you used any of these responses? How helpful was this response?

_____

_____

_____

_____

_____

_____

17

Responding differently

There are often **similarities** between the relationships we have with voices and the relationships we
have with family and friends. If you have any difficult relationships there are things you can do to try
and change them. It doesn't matter if these difficult
relationships are with voices, other people, or both.
If you learn to change one relationship then you
can transfer this learning to other relationships.

Firstly, it is important to identify any relationships
you have that are difficult, and to assess the likeli-
hood of these relationships being able to change.
These relationships might include your relationship
with your voice.

Name of a person/voice I have a difficult relationship with	How difficult is this relationship? On a scale of 0 'not at all difficult' to 10 'extremely difficult'	How likely is this relationship to change? On a scale of 0 'not at all likely' to 10 'extremely likely'

Martin's story

> Martin's difficult relationships:
>
> • Mother = very difficult relationship (7 out of 10) and could be changed (7 out of 10)
>
> • Voice of stepfather = extremely difficult relationship (10 out of 10), but unlikely to change (3 out of 10)
>
> • Sister = moderately difficult relationship (5 out of 10), and could be changed (7 out of 10)

Now you need to decide which relationship you would like to work on. It might be best to choose the one that is most likely to change. There is no right answer as to which one you should choose.

The difficult relationship that I would like to work on is . . .

'My relationship with _____'

In order to better understand the difficult relationship you have chosen to work on it can help to think about the kinds of things the voice/other person says to you. You can use the questions below to remind you of what they say.

Do they . . .

Criticise you?
If yes, write down what
they say:

Call you names?
If yes, write down what
they say:

Talk about your past?
If yes, write down what
they say:

**Tell you
what to do?**
If yes, write
down what
they say:

**Comment
on your
activities?**
If yes, write
down what
they say:

18

Becoming more assertive

You have focused in previous exercises on the way that the voice or other person relates to you – this may have seemed quite natural, but thinking about your role in the relationship may be harder.

We often feel that we have no say in difficult re-lationships – it feels as if the relationships are all one-way traffic from the voice or the other person. But we are playing a role in the relationships – even if it doesn't feel like it.

You can use the table below to explore some of the things that are said to you in the relationship you have chosen to work on and identify how you feel, what you say and how you act in response. You might want to think about specific events, or how things generally are.

They say . . .	I feel . . .	I say . . .	I act by . . .

Q & A

Are there any patterns in the way you respond in this difficult relationship?

_____

_____

_____

_____

_____

_____

How do you think your responses affected
the relationship?

_____

_____

_____

_____

One way to change the relationship is to talk back in a more **assertive** way. This is not the same as being aggressive.

By assertive, we mean standing up for your views – and expressing these views in ways that show respect for both yourself and the voice/other person. Assertiveness involves communicating our feelings and opinions in an **honest** way that promotes a **healthy** view of ourselves and others.

For example, the voice may say something as if it is a fact, such as 'You are useless', but this is only the opinion of the voice, which you have the right to question. You can ask:

- What do **I** think?

- Am I useless all of the time?

- Do I have a different view?

- What **evidence** is there to support my view?

An assertive response would be, 'I hear what you're saying and I do feel useless some of the time – but I don't agree that I'm useless all of the time. Sometimes I do things well and last week I was thanked by a friend for helping them'.

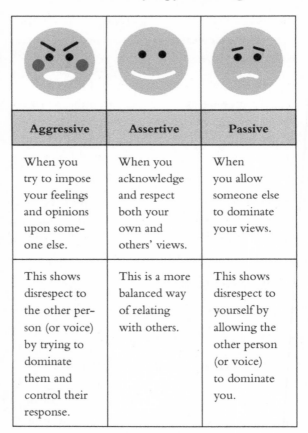

Aggressive	Assertive	Passive
When you try to impose your feelings and opinions upon someone else.	When you acknowledge and respect both your own and others' views.	When you allow someone else to dominate your views.
This shows disrespect to the other person (or voice) by trying to dominate them and control their response.	This is a more balanced way of relating with others.	This shows disrespect to yourself by allowing the other person (or voice) to dominate you.

In order to see what scope there is for you to be more assertive you can re-examine your responses to the voice/other person in the relationship and try to change this to a response that is more respectful to both yourself and to them.

When we are being assertive we will:

---

1. Use 'I' statements

- 'I prefer to . . . '

- 'I would like to . . . '

---

2. Distinguish between fact and opinion

- 'In my opinion . . . '

- 'As I understand it . . . '

---

3. Constructively criticise without condemning

- 'I feel disappointed when you . . . '

- 'I find it unacceptable when you . . . '

You might want to use the table below to think about whether your typical responses are passive, aggressive or assertive. If they aren't assertive try to think of an alternative response that is more assertive.

They say . . .	I respond by . . . (feelings/actions/ what I say)	Is my response: passive, aggressive or assertive?	An assertive response would be . . .		

The next step is to use these assertive responses the next time you are faced with a difficult conversation with the voice/other person.

Martin's story

Martin's assertive response to his voice:

- Martin's voice says, 'If you go out I will punish you.'

- Martin responds by feeling frightened and staying at home.

- Martin's response is passive.

- Martin's assertive response is, 'It's not OK for you to boss me around. I prefer to make my own decisions. I would like to go out.'

Top tip

You might find it helpful to practise your assertive responses with someone you feel comfortable with. One of you could roleplay the person or voice you are trying to respond assertively to.

Q & A

Once you have had a chance to try out your new assertive responses, it can be helpful to take some time to reflect on how this went.

How does it feel when you give the assertive response?

_____

_____

_____

_____

_____

How did the other person feel and respond when you were being assertive?

_____

_____

_____

_____

_____

How was this interaction different to others you have had in the past?

_____

_____

_____

_____

_____

It can be difficult to be assertive at first if this isn't usually how you relate to others. As with all the techniques we have covered so far, it takes practice and time to develop this skill. Becoming assertive will require some perseverance.

When trying to be assertive, you also need to be aware of your **tone** and **loudness** of voice**, gestures** and other **non-verbal** communication. You might think these non-verbal communications are more relevant to speaking with people rather than voices, but we want to get into good habits for all types of relationships so try to use them with your voice as well.

Assertive non-verbal communication involves the *whole* body . . .

Eye contact
Not too much, not too
little.

Facial expressions
Consistent with what
you are saying.

Hand placement
In a resting position,
e.g. on your lap or by
your side.

Voice tone
Steady and warm,
not too loud but
also not quiet.

Breathing
Regular, helping
you to stay as calm
as possible.

Posture
Confident, not
slouched or bolt
upright.

Once you have had a chance to try out your new assertive responses with your assertive non-verbal communication, it can be helpful to take some time to reflect on how this went.

Q & A

How does it feel when you used assertive non-verbal communication?

_____

_____

_____

_____

How did the other person feel and respond when you were being assertive?

_____

_____

_____

_____

_____

How was this interaction different to when you only used assertive statement without the assertive non-verbal communication?

_____

_____

_____

_____

_____

19

Having a different conversation

If you have found the exercises up to now helpful, then try to continue using your assertive statements and the assertive non-verbal communication. You might want to try being assertive in the context of some of the other difficult relationships you identified earlier. Each time you have an assertive conversation, it is important to take the time to review how it went. You can use the table below to help you do this.

They said . . .	My assertive response was . . .	They responded by . . .	This conversation made me feel . . .		

Martin's story

After Martin practised his assertive response:

Martin's voice says, 'If you go out I will punish you.'

Martin's assertive response was, 'It's not OK for you to boss me around. I prefer to make my own decisions. I would like to go out.'

Martin's voice responded by shouting loudly at him.

The conversation made Martin feel anxious, but also determined to stand-up to this bullying voice.

Top tip

Bear in mind that other people and voices may sometimes respond aggressively as they may not like you standing up for yourself. This may be a sign that the other person or voice wants you to return to your old non-assertive ways. Persistence is key!

The other person or voice may try to manipulate you by playing on your weaknesses. You might find it helpful to look at the evidence and experiences that you identified in the Me topic to build your self-esteem. This evidence can be used in the conversation to help build your confidence and enable you to stand up for yourself – even if the other person or voice persists in being difficult.

When responding assertively two things are really important:

1. Practise – it gets a little easier each time you try.

2. Spread your assertiveness to other conversations you have.

If you have found this helpful, then you might want to repeat this process with another of the difficult relationships that you identified. This will involve:

1. Identifying the difficult relationship you want to work on.

2. Coming up with some assertive statements that you could use.

3. Practising using these statements with someone you trust.

4. Trying out these assertive statements with the other person/voice.

5. Remembering to use your assertive non-verbal communication.

6. Taking the time to reflect on how this went. How did it feel? How did the other person/voice respond? Did you notice anything different?

20

Key points

- We can try to change our difficult relationships with our voices and our family and friends. It doesn't matter where we start – positive change in one relationship is likely to have a positive influence on other relationships.

- Once you have decided which relationship you want to change, it is important to investigate the relationship and get to know it as well as you can.

- It is important to notice patterns in the way that you respond within this relationship – are you being aggressive or passive?

- You can change your responses into ones that are assertive – which respect both yourself and the voice/person you are relating to.

- Your assertive responses will need to use clear 'I' statements, and distinguish fact from opinion (for instance, by questioning the accuracy of what is being said to you).

- When you are responding assertively you will also need to be aware of your tone of voice, gestures and non-verbal communication.

- Voices/other people may not appreciate your attempts at being assertive and may respond negatively.

- Practice is important, so be sure to use your assertive responses every time you have conversations with this voice/person.

- As your responses become more assertive you may feel that you have more self-worth and respect for yourself. You may also notice that the voice/other person is being less dominant and intrusive.

Notes

_____

_____

_____

Reflecting on the My Relationships topic

After working through this topic you might find it helpful to take some time to reflect on what you might have learnt. There is space for you to write an answer in relation to each of these questions, as well as space for you to add your own reflections.

How have you found this topic?	What have you learnt from this topic?
_____	_____
_____	_____
_____	_____
_____	_____
_____	_____
_____	_____
What is one good thing you can take away from this topic?	What positive action could you take over the next week?
_____	_____
_____	_____
_____	_____
_____	_____
_____	_____
_____	_____

Personal reflections

_____

_____

_____

_____

_____

_____

Part 5: Looking to the Future

21

Moving forwards

Across the topics in this book we have learnt about different ways to understand and overcome distressing voices. We have seen that hearing voices is not such an unusual experience, and that some people are not particularly distressed by their voices.

Hearing voices itself is not necessarily the problem and the focus of this book has been to overcome the **distress** caused by hearing voices. There is no right way to do this. You can **choose** the ideas that you find most helpful and focus on these.

To overcome distressing voices, we have looked at:

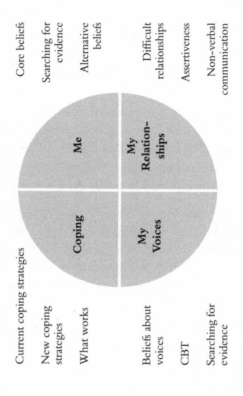

22

Reflections

Now that you have had a chance to try some of the techniques and ideas in the previous topics it might be helpful to think about what you learnt from each of them and what you can take forward into your everyday life.

Q & A

From the **Coping** module, what did you find most helpful?

_____

_____

_____

_____

_____

From the **Me** module, what did you find most helpful?

_____

_____

_____

_____

From the **My Voices** module, what did you find most helpful?

_____

_____

_____

_____

From the **My Relationships** module, what did you find most helpful?

_____

_____

_____

_____

Looking at all of the things you have learnt or found helpful from this book, it is now important to make concrete and specific plans on how you can put it all into practice. If we make these detailed plans, then we are more likely to stick to them.

Firstly, consider what idea from this book you want to put into practice and then use the diagram below to make a detailed plan of how you will do this.

'I am going to _____'

When are you going to do this?

_____

_____

_____

_____

Who are you going to do this with?

_____

_____

_____

_____

Where will you do this?

_____

_____

_____

_____

How can you make sure you do this?

_____

_____

_____

_____

Why is this important to do?

_____

_____

_____

_____

You might find it helpful to create several detailed plans for different ideas that you want to put into practice. Try to be as concrete and specific as possible.

Top tip

Make sure that you take the time to recognise when you have stuck to a plan and give yourself credit for this. The more you practise any of the ideas in this book, the easier they will become.

You might find it helpful to tell your family, friends, or health professionals about your detailed plans so that they can support you and encourage you to stick to the plan.

23

What I want to do!

Once we have begun to overcome distressing voices, this can create room in our lives for doing things that bring us pleasure and a sense of achievement.

You might want to think about the things you would be doing if it wasn't for distressing voices.

If distressing voices were not around I would be . . .

1	
2	
3	
4	
5	

Q & A

Could you be doing any of these things now, even if voices are still around?

If yes, which ones?

_____

_____

_____

_____

_____

_____

_____

Starting to do the things we enjoy or that give us a sense of personal achievement, even if voices are around, can bring about lots of positive outcomes:

- We might find more evidence that the voices don't always have control.

- We might find more evidence that the voices don't always speak the truth.

- We might find more evidence to weaken our negative core beliefs.

- We might find more evidence to strengthen our alternative, more helpful core beliefs.

- We might have more opportunities to practise being assertive.

- We might learn something new.

- We might meet new people.

- We might have a good time.

> **Top tip**

When you try doing something that voices have stopped you doing in the past, take a moment to reflect on what was positive about the experience – if you notice some positive outcomes, then why not do it again?

Step 1:

Step 2:

Step 3:

Step 4:

Goal!

24

Your goal

You may have felt that the things you would be doing if voices weren't around are too difficult at the moment. It might be helpful to break down these ideas into smaller steps.

For example, if you write, 'Get a paid job,' but this feels too difficult at the moment, then a first step might be looking for voluntary work.

What steps can you take in moving towards your goal?

'My goal is to _____

_____

_____.'

Top tip

You might need more than five steps to reach your goal. Feel free to add in additional steps – just make sure that each step is moving you **toward** your goal.

Other resources

> Hearing voices does not have to be a
> barrier to doing the things that we want
> to do in our lives.

There are lots of other resources out there that you
can access that you might find helpful to overcome
distressing voices.

Below is a list of some of the organisations, websites
and books you might find useful.

Organisations and websites

British Association for Behavioural and Cognitive Psychotherapies (BABCP)

BABCP is the lead organisation for CBT in the UK.
Here you can find details of all officially accredited
cognitive behaviour therapists.

Website: www.babcp.com

Hearing Voices Network (HVN) (UK)

HVN offers information, support and understanding to people who hear voices and those who support them, e.g. promoting, developing and supporting self-help groups. They have a telephone helpline: 0114 271 8210.

Website: www.hearing-voices.org

Email: nhvn@hotmail.co.uk

Healthtalk

Healthtalkonline is the award-winning website of DIPEx, a charity that lets you share in thousands of experiences of more than sixty health-related conditions and illnesses. You can watch videos or listen to audio clips of interviews with people who hear voices.

Website: www.healthtalkonline.org/
mental_health/Experiences_of_psychosis/
Topic/3934/

International Society for Psychological and Social Approaches to Psychosis (ISPS)

ISPS promotes psychological treatments for people who experience psychosis (e.g. hallucinations and delusions) and greater understanding of the psychological and social causes of psychosis.

Website: www.isps.org

Intervoice

Intervoice is the International Community for Hearing Voices. It undertakes training, education and research. Online resources include a discussion forum and links to hearing voices groups worldwide.

Website: www.intervoiceonline.org

Is Anyone Else Like Me?

Is anyone else like me? is a website that was create as part of the EYE research project. The site has been created in collaboration with young people who have experience of psychosis. The website was designed to help young people engage in early intervention in psychosis services, but has lots of useful information and resources that are applicable to anyone who has unusual experiences.

Website: www.isanyoneelselikeme.org.uk/

Downloadable booklets: www.isanyoneelselikeme.org.uk/info/booklets

MIND

Mind helps people to take control over their mental health by providing information and advice, training programmes, grants and services through a network of local Mind associations.

Website: www.mind.org.uk

National Institute for Health and Clinical Excellence (NICE)

NICE uses the best available research evidence to make recommendations to the NHS about treatments. Recommendations about CBT for schizophrenia were published in 2002 and 2009.

Website: www.nice.org.uk

Rethink Mental Illness

A UK national charity that believes a better life is possible for millions of people affected by mental illness. Their website and helplines give information and advice.

Website: www.rethink.org

YouTube videos

At YouTube you can search for: 'The Voices in My Head' Eleanor Longden – TED Talks; 'Jacqui Dillon: Beyond the Therapy Room' and 'IIMHN Conference 2016 – Peter Bullimore's Story'.

Website: www.youtube.com

Books

Assertiveness and mood

Assertiveness: Step by Step, Windy Dryden and Daniel Constantinon, 2004, London: Sheldon Press

Mind over Mood: Change How You Feel by Changing the Way You Think, Dennis Greenberger and Christine A. Padesky, (second ed.), London: Guildford Press

Overcoming . . . series

Overcoming Anger and Irritability, William Davies, 2016 (second ed.), London: Robinson

Overcoming Anxiety, Helen Kennerley, 2014 (second ed.), London: Robinson

Overcoming Depression, Paul Gilbert, 2009 (third ed.), London: Robinson

Overcoming Distressing Voices, Mark Hayward, Clara Strauss and David Kingdon, 2018 (second ed.), London: Robinson

Overcoming Low Self-Esteem, Melanie Fennell, 2016 (second ed.), London: Robinson

Overcoming Paranoid and Suspicious Thoughts, Daniel Freeman, Philippa Garety and Jason Freeman, 2016 (second ed.), London: Robinson

Psychosis

Back to Life, Back to Normality: Cognitive Therapy, Recovery and Psychosis, Douglas Turkington, David Kingdom et al., 2009, Cambridge: Cambridge University Press

Madness Explained: Psychosis and Human Nature, Richard P. Bentall, 2003, London: Penguin

Voicing Carer Experiences, Ruth Chandler, Simon Bradstreet and Mark Hayward (eds), 2012, Scottish Recovery Network

Voicing Psychotic Experiences: A Reconsideration of Recovery and Diversity, Ruth Chandler and Mark Hayward (eds), 2009, Brighton: OLM/Pavilion

Voices

Accepting Voices, Marius Romme and Sandra Escher, 1993, London: MIND Publications

Making Sense of Voices, Marius Romme and Sandra Escher, 2000, London: MIND Publications

Living with Voices: 50 Stories of Recovery, Marius Romme, Sandra Escher, et al., 2009, Ross-on-Wye: PCCS Books

Diary

Take the time to think about what you have learnt during the past week, and choose one thing you would like to try next week to make a positive change. You can use this diary to monitor your progress over the week.

'My goal for this week is to:

_____

_____

_____,

Monday

Tuesday

Wednesday

Thursday

Friday

Saturday

Sunday

An Introduction to Coping with Insomnia and Sleep Problems

2nd Edition

Colin A. Espie

ISBN: 978-1-47213-854-5 (paperback)
ISBN: 978-1-47213-892-7 (ebook)

Poor sleep can have a huge impact on our health and well-being, leaving us feeling run-down, exhausted and stressed out. Written by a leading expert in the field, this simple guide explains the causes of insomnia and why it is so difficult to break bad habits. It gives you clinically proven cognitive behavioural therapy (CBT) techniques for improving the quality of your sleep, showing you how to keep a sleep diary, set personal goals, improve your sleep hygiene, deal with a racing mind and make lasting improvements to your sleeping and waking pattern.